MW01629195

This book is dedicated to my mom
for all of the lives she has touched
through education.

-Lacretia

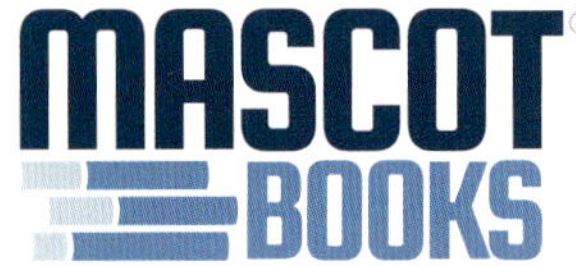

www.mascotbooks.com

Billy the Bully

For more information, please contact:
Mascot Books
560 Herndon Parkway #120
Herndon, VA 20170
info@mascotbooks.com

Library of Congress Control Number: 2014917879

CPSIA Code: PRT1114A
ISBN-13: 978-1-62086-940-6

Printed in the United States

BILLY THE BULLY

To Arlene
Wishing you abundant
Health and Success!
Lacretia Palmer
5/11/17
xoxo

Lacretia Palmer

illustrated by

Romney Vasquez

NOTE TO THE READER

We all talk about how important nutrition is, but we never talk about what happens when it's taken away from us. I would like for the focus of my book to be on how to deal with bullying at a Nutrition level. My goal is to raise awareness of this situation and also to teach children the difference between right and wrong.

"Wake up, Billy!

It's time to get
ready for school,"

said Billy's mom.

Those were the words
Billy loved to hear.

Billy jumped
out of bed and
washed his face,

brushed his teeth,
and got dressed.

After another shout from
his mom downstairs, Billy
raced down to the kitchen.

"Mom, I'm not hungry. I'll just eat at school," said Billy.

"Okay, Billy, but you know Nancy is going to tell you how important **nutrition** is."
COCO FLAKES
TO DO
"I know, Mom. I'll just deal with that when I see her. Now come on! I'm going to be late for school."

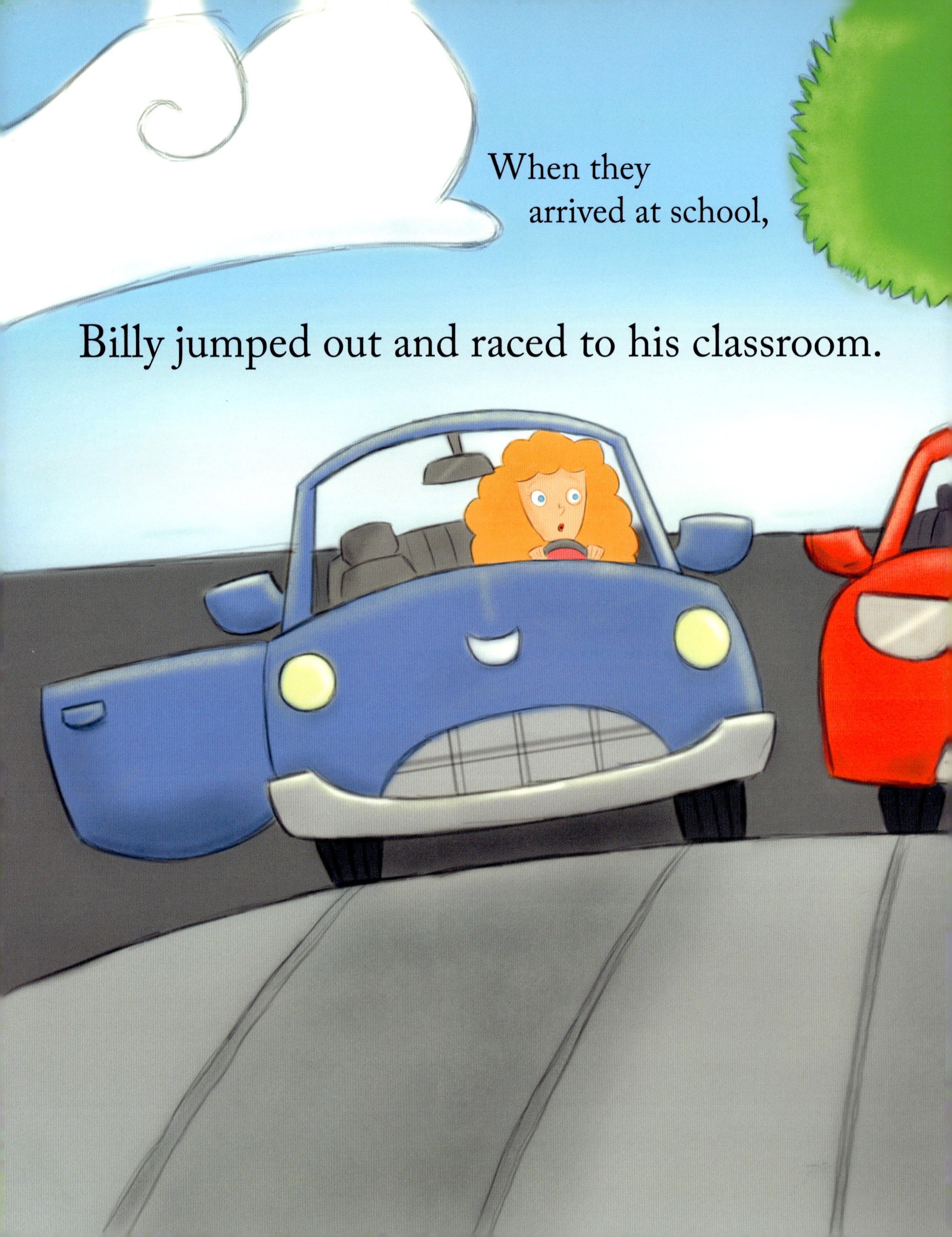

When they
arrived at school,

Billy jumped out and raced to his classroom.

He was so excited
for the day he forgot
to tell his mother goodbye.

Just like that, it was almost
Billy's favorite time of the day...
LUNCHTIME!
BILLY
RULEZ!

With the lunch bell moments away from ringing, all of the kids were excited to see what was on the day's lunch menu. But there was one problem...

BILLY THE BULLY.

As the kids walked to the cafeteria, Munchin' Mario said, "He won't eat my lunch because I shove all of my food in my face."

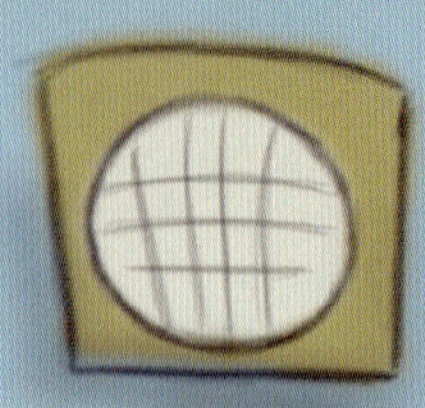

Simple Sara added,

"I don't care whose lunch he takes."

Without hesitation, Sharing Samantha offered, "Whoever's lunch he does take, I will share my food with them."

On his way to the cafeteria, **BILLY THE BULLY** saw a boy sitting on the benches, about to eat his sandwich.

Billy hovered over him with a threatening glare.

The timid boy handed Billy the sandwich and ran away.

Samantha caught up with the boy and gave him half of her lunch.

He mumbled a quick

"thank you"

before scarfing down the meal.

After finishing the sandwich, Billy spotted a group of girls.

he threatened.

They timidly handed over their cookies. Billy set out to steal more food. Billy noticed his peers at a nearby table and quickly made his way toward them. Munchin' Mario, Simple Sara, and Nutritious Nancy grew quiet as he approached.

Billy asked,

"What's wrong?"

"Billy, I have talked to you about bullying kids for their lunch in the past," said Nancy.

As always,
Billy responded with,
"Yeah,
yeah,
yeah."

One day, Billy's little brother, Bobby, came home from school crying.

"What's wrong Bobby?"

asked Billy.

Bobby responded, "Some kid has been taking my lunch all week and I'm so hungry!"

Finally, **BILLY THE BULLY** understood why he shouldn't take his classmates' lunches. Billy knew what he had to do.

The next day, Billy went to school hoping to talk to all of the kids whose lunches he had stolen.

The only problem was, **he couldn't remember who he had stolen from, he had taken so many lunches!**

Then, inspiration struck. Billy decided to post a banner at school that said, "If you've ever been bullied by Billy for your lunch, please come to a picnic on Saturday at noon at Mayberry Park."

After school, Billy went home to inform his parents of what he'd done.

His parents couldn't believe that Billy was a bully! Billy asked if they could help him host a picnic to give back the lunches he took from all the kids. Even though they were disappointed in Billy, they were proud that he wanted to make it right.

Billy and his family spent all Friday evening preparing for the picnic.

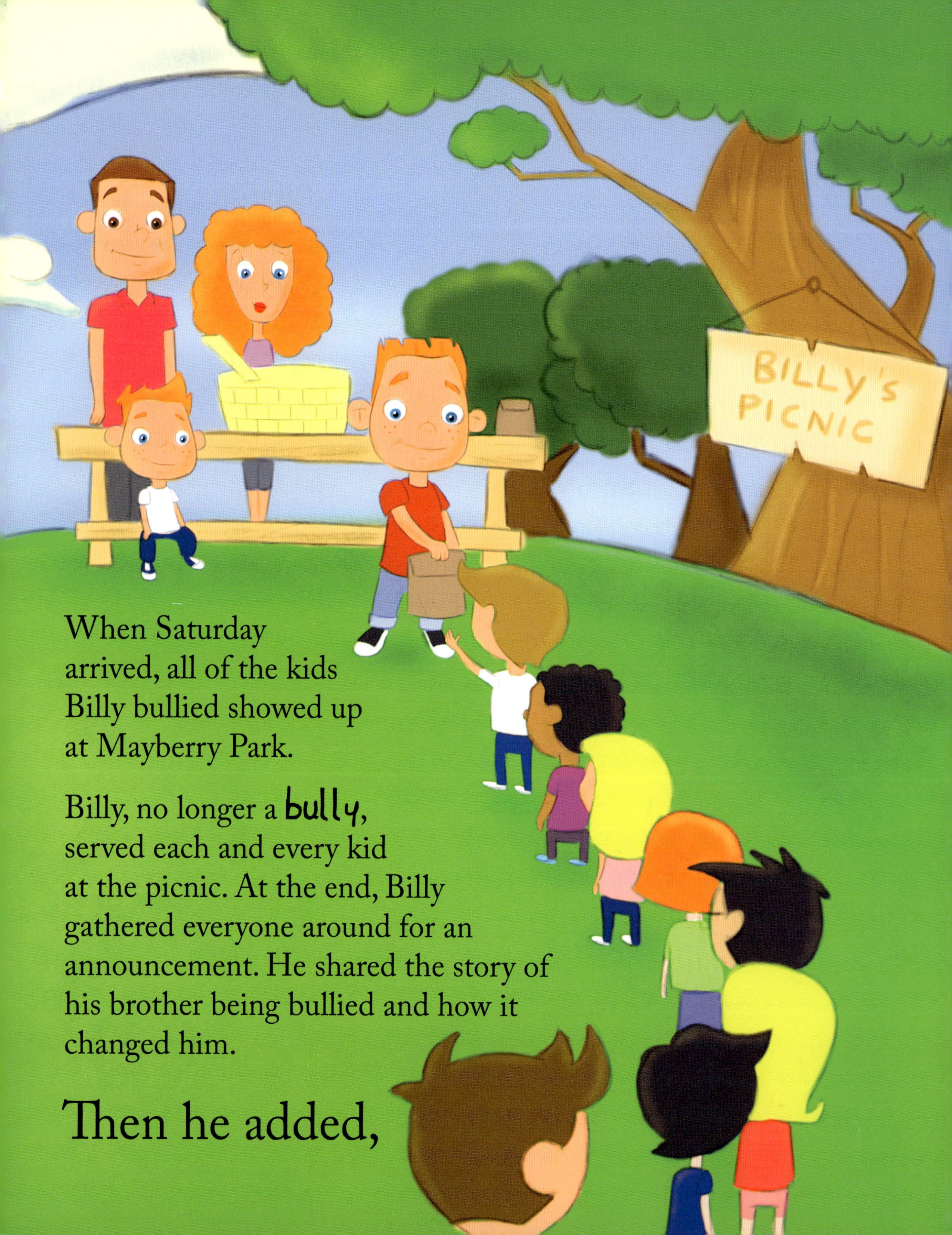

When Saturday arrived, all of the kids Billy bullied showed up at Mayberry Park.

Billy, no longer a **bully**, served each and every kid at the picnic. At the end, Billy gathered everyone around for an announcement. He shared the story of his brother being bullied and how it changed him.

Then he added,

"I AM NO LONGER A BULLY!"

What motivated Billy to change?

ABOUT THE AUTHOR

I remember this form of bullying taking place when I was a child. However, I didn't want to share my thoughts with just my family, friends, and coworkers, but with people across the country. I believe speaking on this issue will in turn contribute to making the world a better place.